AI Unveiled for The Beginner: Navigating the New Frontier of Intelligence

AI Unveiled for The Beginner: Navigating the New Frontier of Intelligence

(Learn How Artificial Intelligence is Transforming Our World and What It Means for You as we Explore the Future, Ethics, and Impact of Artificial Intelligence on Society.)

DR. Selva Sugunendran

CEng, MIEE, MCMI, CHt, MIMDHA, MBBNLP, MGONLP

#1 Best Selling Author, Speaker & Coach

© www.AIRoboticsForGood.com

Copyright © 2024 by DR. Selva
AI UNVEILER FOR THE BEGINNER

Navigating the Challenges of Caring for Caregivers in a Home Setting

All rights reserved. No part of this book may be reproduced or transmitted in any form or by any means, electronic or mechanical, including photocopying, recording, or by any information storage and retrieval system, without permission in writing from the Copyright owner.

Medical Disclaimer: The author of this book is a competent, experienced writer. He has taken every opportunity to ensure that all information presented here is correct and up to date at the time of writing. No documentation within this book has been evaluated by the Food and Drug Administration, and no documentation should be used to diagnose, treat, cure, or prevent any disease.

Any information is to be used for educational and information purposes only. It should never be substituted for the medical advice from your doctor or other health care professionals.
We do not dispense medical advice, prescribe drugs or diagnose any illnesses with our literature.

The author and publisher are not responsible or liable for any self or third-party diagnosis made by visitors based upon the content of this book. The author or publisher does not in any way endorse any commercial products or services linked from other websites to this book.

Please, always consult your doctor or health care specialist if you are in any way concerned about your physical wellbeing.

Contents

(This structure of 12 Chapters is designed to provide a comprehensive overview of artificial intelligence, making it accessible and engaging for a wide audience, while also diving deep into the revolutionary potential and challenges presented by AI, including a special focus on ChatGPT 4.0.).

Foreword viii

Introduction xiii

    Introduction: Embarking on the AI Odyssey xiii
    Why This Journey Matters... xiv
    What Lies Ahead xv
    A Call to Engage.. xvi
    Welcome to the AI Odyssey xvi

Chapter 1: The AI Revolution 1

    The Dawn of a New Era 1
    What is Artificial Intelligence?... 2
    The Impact of AI on Society 3
    Navigating the AI Revolution 4

Chapter 2: How AI Works... 5

    Understanding the Machinery of Intelligence........................... 6
    The Neural Networks 6
    Algorithms: The Brains Behind AI.. 7
    Beyond the Basics 7

Chapter 3: AI in Everyday Life 9

    The Invisible Hand 9
    Transforming Industries 9

AI and Creativity 10
Navigating the AI Landscape 10

Chapter 4: The Building Blocks of AI 13

The Foundation of Intelligence 14
Data: The Fuel for AI 14
Algorithms: The Brains of AI 14
Hardware: The Muscle Behind AI 15

Chapter 5: AI and the Future of Work 17

Navigating the Changing Landscape 17
Skills for the AI-Powered Workplace 18
The Role of Policy in Shaping the Future of Work 18

Chapter 6: Ethical Considerations in AI 21

The Moral Compass of AI 21
Bias and Fairness 22
Privacy in the Age of AI 22
Accountability and Transparency 23

Chapter 7: The AI Alignment Problem 25

Aligning AI with Human Values 25
Risks of Misaligned AI 25
Strategies for AI Alignment 26
The Future of AI Alignment 26

Chapter 8: ChatGPT 4.0: A Case Study 27

Unveiling ChatGPT 4.0 27
How ChatGPT 4.0 Works 28
Applications and Impact 28
Ethical and Societal Considerations 29

Chapter 9: Superintelligence and Beyond 31

The Path to Superintelligence 32
Potential Impacts and Scenarios 32
Navigating the Risks 32

Envisioning a Coexistent Future 33

Chapter 10: AI in Governance and Society **35**

The Path to Superintelligence 35
Potential Impacts and Scenarios 36
Navigating the Risks 36
Envisioning a Coexistent Future 36
Governing AI for the Common Good 37
Ethical Governance and Surveillance 37
The Future of Democratic Participation 38

Chapter 11: Preparing for an AI Future **39**

Lifelong Learning in the Age of AI 39
Policy Recommendations for a Sustainable AI Future 41
Conclusion 42

Chapter 12: Embracing AI: A Call to Action **45**

Overcoming AI Anxiety 45
Public Engagement and AI Literacy 46
Visioning a Collaborative Future 47
Conclusion 48

Conclusions **49**

Conclusions: Navigating the AI Horizon 49
Reflecting on the AI Journey 50
Key Insights and Takeaways 52
Looking Forward: The Role of AI in Our Future 53
A Call to Action 54
The 21 Frequently Asked Questions for Beginners to AI 58
Short Answers To The 21 Faqs 60

More Comprehensive Answers to The 21 Faqs **69**

Glossary of AI Technology **121**

Foreword

At the Dawn of an AI-Infused Era

In the grand tapestry of human achievement, few threads are as vibrant and transformative as the development of artificial intelligence. We stand at a pivotal moment in history, a juncture where technology and imagination converge to redefine the boundaries of what's possible. This book is more than a guide; it's a beacon, illuminating the path forward in an era increasingly shaped by AI. As you prepare to navigate its pages, you are embarking on an odyssey that explores the most profound technological revolution of our time.

The creation and evolution of AI represent a mirror reflecting our deepest aspirations, fears, and the unyielding pursuit of knowledge. It's a journey that stretches from the ancient dream of automata to the modern quest for machines that think, learn, and create. The narrative of AI is not just about circuits, algorithms, and data; it's about humanity's relentless quest to understand the essence of intelligence itself.

This book arrives at a critical moment, as we grapple with the opportunities and challenges presented by AI. It offers not just insight but also vision, encouraging us to contemplate our role as stewards of this powerful technology. The chapters within provide a comprehensive exploration of AI, demystifying its complexities and highlighting its potential to enhance our lives, reshape our societies, and address some of our most pressing global challenges.

Yet, for all its potential, AI also poses significant ethical and philosophical questions. It compels us to consider the kind of future we wish to create. As you delve into this book, you'll be invited to ponder these questions, to engage in a dialogue that is crucial for ensuring that AI serves the greater good. This is a conversation that transcends technological circles, encompassing policymakers, educators, entrepreneurs, and, most importantly, everyday citizens.

The authors have embarked on a monumental task, crafting a narrative that is both enlightening and accessible. They have succeeded in creating a work that serves as a compass for navigating the AI landscape, offering clarity and insight into a topic that touches all our lives. Through this book, you are invited to join a community of thinkers, dreamers, and doers who are shaping the future of artificial intelligence.

As we stand on the brink of this new frontier, let this book inspire you to look beyond the horizon, to dream boldly about the possibilities that AI offers. The future of artificial intelligence is not just a tale of technology; it is the story of humanity itself. It is a story that we are writing together, at this very moment.

Let this book be your guide as we embark on this extraordinary journey. May it inspire you to contribute to a future where AI amplifies our human potential, enriches our lives, and leads us toward a more just, sustainable, and flourishing world.

Welcome to the dawn of the AI-infused era. The journey ahead is one of discovery, challenge, and unparalleled opportunity. Let us embrace it with open minds, compassionate hearts, and the unwavering belief that our collective ingenuity can guide us toward a brighter future.

Stephanie Hall

Introduction

"I do believe that crafting an introduction for a book on artificial intelligence that encapsulates the essence of the forthcoming journey while igniting curiosity and enthusiasm in readers is essential. The introduction sets the stage for an engaging exploration of AI, its impacts, and its potential.

This introduction aims to captivate readers' curiosity, setting the stage for a deep and nuanced exploration of artificial intelligence. It positions the book as a guide and companion in the collective endeavour to understand and shape the impact of AI on society."

Introduction: Embarking on the AI Odyssey

Welcome to a journey unlike any other—a voyage through the realms of artificial intelligence, where the future meets the present, and the boundaries of human ingenuity are continually expanded. Whether you are a curious novice, a seasoned professional, or simply an inquisitive mind pondering the ramifications of AI on our society, this book is for you. It's an exploration designed to demystify AI, to uncover its potentials and perils, and to understand its profound impact on our lives and our collective future.

Why This Journey Matters

Artificial intelligence is no longer a distant frontier of science fiction; it is an integral part of our daily lives. From the smartphones in our pockets to the algorithms curating our digital experiences, AI shapes the way we live, work, and interact with the world around us. Yet, for many, AI remains an elusive and misunderstood force—an array of complex technologies with uncertain implications for society.

This book aims to bridge that gap, offering a window into the world of AI that is accessible, engaging, and thought-provoking. It seeks to equip you with the knowledge to navigate the AI landscape, to understand its dynamics, and to engage with its ethical and societal challenges. In doing so, this book endeavours to inspire a conversation about the role of AI in our future—a dialogue that is inclusive, informed, and grounded in a shared vision for harnessing AI for the betterment of humanity.

What Lies Ahead

As you turn these pages, you will embark on a comprehensive exploration of artificial intelligence, from its foundational principles to the cutting-edge developments shaping its future. You will discover how AI works, the ways it is transforming industries and societies, and the challenges it poses to ethics and governance. Through the lens of AI, we will examine broader questions about intelligence, creativity, and the future of human work.

This book will also introduce you to the latest advancements in AI technology, such as ChatGPT 4.0, and delve into the philosophical debates surrounding Superintelligence and the alignment problem. By weaving together insights from experts, case studies, and ethical discussions, we aim to provide a holistic view of AI's role in our world.

A Call to Engage

More than just a text to be read, this book is an invitation to engage with one of the most significant forces shaping the 21st century. It is a call to reflect on our values, to question the direction of technological progress, and to actively participate in shaping a future where AI amplifies our human potential rather than diminishing it.

As we stand at the crossroads of a new era, the choices we make today will echo through generations. This book is not just about understanding AI; it's about envisioning and working toward a future that reflects our collective aspirations, ethics, and spirit of innovation.

Welcome to the AI Odyssey

So, I invite you to join me on this odyssey through the world of artificial intelligence. Together, let's explore the wonders and warnings of AI, armed with curiosity and a critical mind. The journey ahead is both exhilarating and daunting, but it is one we must undertake with open eyes and hearts ready to shape the future.

Welcome to the exploration of AI—a journey into the heart of our technological age, where we'll discover not just the machines that are changing our world, but also what it means to be human in the age of artificial intelligence.

Chapter 1: The AI Revolution

In this first chapter we'll focus on creating a compelling, informative narrative that appeals to a broad, non-technical audience. Given the format here, I'll begin with "The AI Revolution." This will serve as a foundational piece, setting the tone and approach for subsequent chapters.

The Dawn of a New Era

Artificial Intelligence (AI) is not just a product of the modern digital age but a culmination of human curiosity and ingenuity that spans centuries. From ancient myths of mechanical servants to the pioneering computational theories of the 20th century, the quest to create intelligent machines has long been intertwined with our understanding of what it means to be intelligent. Today, we stand at the precipice of a new era, where AI's impact is not confined to research labs and tech companies but permeates every aspect of our lives.

What is Artificial Intelligence?

At its core, Artificial Intelligence is the science and engineering of making intelligent machines, especially intelligent computer programs. It is related to the similar task of using computers to understand human intelligence, but AI does not have to confine itself to methods that are biologically observable. This definition, first coined by AI pioneer John McCarthy, encapsulates the broad ambition of AI: to replicate or simulate human intelligence in machines.

However, AI is more than just a technical discipline. It is a mirror reflecting our understanding of ourselves and our place in the universe. By attempting to model how we think, learn, and make decisions, AI challenges us to reconsider what it means to be intelligent and how intelligence can be manifested beyond the organic brain.

The Impact of AI on Society

The impact of AI on society has been profound and multifaceted. In its early days, AI was the realm of science fiction and speculative thought experiments. However, the rapid advancement of computing power, data analytics, and machine learning algorithms in the past few decades has catapulted AI from the pages of novels into the fabric of everyday life.

In healthcare, AI algorithms assist doctors in diagnosing diseases with greater accuracy and speed than ever before. In finance, AI systems manage investments, detect fraud, and streamline operations. Autonomous vehicles promise to reshape transportation, while smart assistants like Siri, Alexa, and Google Assistant are becoming commonplace in homes around the world.

Yet, the influence of AI extends beyond practical applications. It challenges our societal norms, ethics, and governance structures. Questions about privacy, surveillance, job displacement, and decision-making autonomy are at the forefront of public discourse, urging us to reconsider the balance between technological progress and human values.

Navigating the AI Revolution

As we navigate this AI revolution, it is imperative to foster a society that is informed, engaged, and proactive. Understanding AI is not just for computer scientists and tech entrepreneurs; it is essential for everyone. By demystifying AI, we can demystify the future—making it less a matter of fate and more a matter of choice.

This chapter sets the stage for a journey through the world of artificial intelligence. As we delve deeper into the subsequent chapters, we will explore the inner workings of AI, its applications, challenges, and the ethical dilemmas it presents. Our goal is not merely to understand AI but to equip ourselves with the knowledge to actively shape its role in society.

Together, let's embark on this journey of discovery, reflection, and action. The AI revolution is not just about technology; it's about the future we choose to create.

Chapter 2: How AI Works

This chapter initiates the discussion on AI, its implications, and its significance in the modern world, setting a solid foundation for deeper exploration in the following chapters. Continuing with this momentum, each chapter will unravel another aspect of AI, building towards a comprehensive understanding that empowers readers to engage with Given the platform constraints and the in-depth nature of each chapter, I'll provide a condensed outline and brief introduction for the next two chapters. This approach allows us to maintain a focus on delivering quality content that's engaging and informative, within a manageable scope for each chapter.

Understanding the Machinery of Intelligence

The journey into the world of AI is akin to peeling back the layers of a complex, intricately designed machine. At its heart, AI is about mimicking the processes of human intelligence, but how exactly does it achieve this feat? This chapter delves into the basics of AI and machine learning, shedding light on the algorithms and neural networks that serve as the building blocks of intelligent systems.

The Neural Networks

Imagine the human brain, a dense network of neurons, each playing a crucial role in processing information and making decisions. Neural networks in AI attempt to replicate this biological network digitally, creating systems that can learn from data, recognize patterns, and make decisions with minimal human intervention. We'll explore how these networks are structured and how they evolve through learning, providing a glimpse into the engine that powers AI.

Algorithms: The Brains Behind AI

Algorithms are the brains of AI, the step-by-step instructions that guide machines in performing tasks, from simple calculations to complex decision-making processes. By understanding algorithms, we unlock the secrets to how machines learn from data, adapt to new information, and improve over time. This chapter introduces the types of algorithms that underpin AI, from supervised and unsupervised learning to reinforcement learning, and explains their role in developing intelligent systems.

Beyond the Basics

As we conclude this chapter, we'll touch upon the advanced concepts that are pushing the boundaries of AI, including deep learning, generative models, and more. These technologies are not only enhancing the capabilities of AI but also broadening its applications, impacting fields ranging from medicine to environmental science.

This exploration into the workings of AI demystifies the technology, revealing the remarkable ingenuity and complexity of intelligent systems. As we move forward, we'll see how these technologies are applied in real-world scenarios, transforming industries and daily life.

Chapter 3: AI in Everyday Life

The Invisible Hand

Artificial intelligence has quietly woven itself into the fabric of our daily lives, becoming an invisible hand that guides, assists, and sometimes decides for us. From the moment we wake up to the algorithms that curate our newsfeeds, to the smart devices that manage our homes, AI's presence is ubiquitous and growing. This chapter explores the various ways AI impacts our daily routines, often without our explicit notice.

Transforming Industries

The transformative power of AI is not limited to personal convenience but extends across all sectors of the economy. In healthcare, AI assists in diagnosing diseases with precision, offering new hope for treatments. In finance, it navigates the complexities of markets, managing risks, and uncovering opportunities. The transportation sector stands on the cusp of a revolution with autonomous vehicles, promising safer, more efficient travel. We'll examine these transformations, highlighting the benefits and challenges they bring.

AI and Creativity

One of the most fascinating developments in AI is its foray into creative fields, challenging the notion that creativity is a uniquely human attribute. From generating art and music to writing stories, AI's creative endeavors are not only expanding the boundaries of what machines can do but also prompting us to reconsider the nature of creativity itself. This chapter will delve into examples of AI's creative output and discuss its implications for artists and creative industries.

Navigating the AI Landscape

As we navigate through the myriad ways AI influences our lives, it's essential to remain informed and critical. The convenience and efficiencies AI brings are accompanied by challenges and ethical considerations, from privacy concerns to the potential for bias in decision-making. By understanding AI's role in our daily lives, we can better advocate for technologies that enhance our society while safeguarding our values.

This chapter not only illuminates the pervasiveness of AI in our daily lives but also sets the stage for deeper discussions on its societal implications, ethical considerations, and the future we aspire to create in harmony with intelligent machines.

Chapter 4: The Building Blocks of AI

Continuing in this vein for subsequent chapters would involve a blend of technical insight, practical examples, and philosophical reflection, ensuring the book remains accessible, engaging, and thought-provoking for a non-technical audience. and influence the AI-driven future.

Creating a detailed narrative for each chapter while ensuring it remains concise and engaging for readers is a challenging task. For the sake of brevity and to maintain the quality of content, I'll provide summarized introductions for the next two chapters, Chapter 4: "The Building Blocks of AI" and Chapter 5: "AI and the Future of Work". These summaries aim to highlight key concepts and issues, laying the groundwork for a deeper exploration of each topic within the book.

The Foundation of Intelligence

To truly grasp how artificial intelligence operates, one must understand its foundation—data, algorithms, and the hardware that powers it. This chapter demystifies these core components, explaining how they come together to create systems capable of learning, reasoning, and acting in ways that mimic human intelligence.

Data: The Fuel for AI

Data is the lifeblood of artificial intelligence. It's what AI systems learn from, making it possible for them to recognize patterns, make predictions, and improve over time. This section explores the types of data AI uses, how it's collected and processed, and the critical role of data quality and quantity in the effectiveness of AI applications.

Algorithms: The Brains of AI

Algorithms are the step-by-step instructions that guide AI systems in their tasks. This part of the chapter delves into the different types of machine learning algorithms, including supervised, unsupervised, and reinforcement learning. Readers will gain insight into how these algorithms learn from data, adapt to new situations, and make decisions.

Hardware: The Muscle Behind AI

The incredible capabilities of AI wouldn't be possible without the powerful hardware that supports it. This section introduces the processors and computing architectures that underpin AI research and applications, from GPUs to specialized AI chips. We'll explore how advancements in hardware are accelerating AI development and enabling more sophisticated applications.

By understanding the building blocks of AI, readers will appreciate the complexities and challenges of creating intelligent systems. This foundation is crucial for anyone looking to engage with AI, whether as a user, developer, or critic.

Chapter 5: AI and the Future of Work

The advent of AI is transforming the workplace, automating routine tasks, and creating new opportunities for human workers. This chapter examines the impact of AI on the job market, debunking myths about job displacement, and highlighting the emergence of new roles and industries in the AI era.

Navigating the Changing Landscape

Automation: Threat or Opportunity?

Automation, powered by AI, is often seen as a threat to jobs. However, this section argues that automation can be an opportunity for growth and innovation. By taking over mundane tasks, AI allows humans to focus on more creative and strategic activities. We'll explore case studies where automation has led to enhanced productivity and job creation.

Skills for the AI-Powered Workplace

As AI reshapes industries, the demand for certain skills is changing. This part of the chapter identifies the skills that will be most valuable in an AI-driven future, including technical literacy, problem-solving, creativity, and emotional intelligence. We'll provide guidance on how individuals and organizations can prepare for the transition, emphasizing the importance of lifelong learning and adaptability.

The Role of Policy in Shaping the Future of Work

The final section discusses the role of government and organizational policies in ensuring a smooth transition to an AI-powered economy. Topics include retraining programs, social safety nets, and ethical guidelines for AI use in the workplace. By addressing these policy issues, we can mitigate the challenges posed by AI and harness its potential to create a more prosperous and inclusive future.

These chapters aim to provide readers with a comprehensive understanding of AI's fundamental components and its profound impact on the workforce. As we progress through the book, we'll continue to explore the ethical, societal, and technical challenges and opportunities presented by AI, empowering readers to navigate the AI revolution with knowledge and confidence.

Chapter 6: Ethical Considerations in AI

Continuing with the structure and approach we've established, let's provide introductory frameworks for Chapter 6: "Ethical Considerations in AI" and Chapter 7: "The AI Alignment Problem." These chapters delve into the complex moral landscapes and technical challenges of AI, fostering a deeper understanding of the responsibilities and potential solutions that come with advancing AI technologies.

The Moral Compass of AI

As AI becomes increasingly integral to our lives, its ethical implications come into sharper focus. This chapter examines the ethical considerations that arise as AI systems make decisions that affect human lives, from privacy concerns to questions of fairness and accountability.

Bias and Fairness

Bias in AI systems reflects biases present in their training data, leading to unfair outcomes in various applications like hiring, law enforcement, and lending. We'll explore how biases are introduced into AI systems, the consequences of such biases, and the ongoing efforts to develop more fair and equitable AI technologies.

Privacy in the Age of AI

AI's ability to analyse vast amounts of personal data raises significant privacy concerns. This section discusses the balance between leveraging data for beneficial AI applications and ensuring individuals' privacy rights are respected, including a look at regulations like GDPR and the ethical design of AI systems.

Accountability and Transparency

As AI systems become more autonomous, determining accountability for their actions becomes increasingly complex. This part addresses the challenges in ensuring AI systems are transparent and explainable, enabling humans to understand, predict, and control AI behaviours, and the importance of establishing clear guidelines and mechanisms for accountability.

Chapter 7: The AI Alignment Problem

Aligning AI with Human Values

The AI alignment problem refers to the challenge of ensuring AI systems' goals and behaviours are aligned with human values and interests. This chapter introduces the concept, its significance, and why solving it is critical for the safe and beneficial development of AI technologies.

Risks of Misaligned AI

Misaligned AI can lead to unintended and potentially harmful consequences, especially as AI systems become more powerful. We'll discuss examples of alignment failures, the potential risks associated with advanced AI systems, and the importance of proactive measures to prevent such outcomes.

Strategies for AI Alignment

This section explores various approaches to solving the alignment problem, from technical solutions like reward modelling and iterative training to broader strategies involving stakeholder engagement and regulatory frameworks. The goal is to highlight the multidisciplinary effort required to align AI with human ethics and values.

The Future of AI Alignment

Looking ahead, the chapter concludes with a discussion on the ongoing research and debate in the field of AI alignment, the role of international cooperation, and the importance of public awareness and engagement in shaping the future direction of AI development.

These chapters aim to provide readers with a nuanced understanding of the ethical dilemmas and alignment challenges that accompany the advancement of AI technologies. By highlighting these issues and exploring potential solutions, the book encourages a proactive and informed approach to navigating the ethical landscapes of AI.

Chapter 8: ChatGPT 4.0: A Case Study

Let's proceed with the foundational sketches for Chapters 8 and 9, focusing on "ChatGPT 4.0: A Case Study" and "Superintelligence and Beyond," respectively. These chapters aim to offer insights into specific AI advancements and the broader implications for future developments, emphasizing the practical applications, challenges, and ethical considerations of cutting-edge AI technologies.

Unveiling ChatGPT 4.0

This chapter introduces ChatGPT 4.0, a state-of-the-art language model developed by Open AI. It outlines the technological advancements from previous versions and how these improvements have expanded its capabilities in understanding and generating human-like text, making it a versatile tool for a wide range of applications.

How ChatGPT 4.0 Works

An exploration into the inner workings of ChatGPT 4.0 provides readers with a glimpse into the complex algorithms and neural network architectures that underpin its ability to process and produce language. This section demystifies the technology, explaining in accessible terms how the model is trained and how it generates responses.

Applications and Impact

ChatGPT 4.0's versatility is showcased through a variety of applications, from writing assistance and customer service to education and creative arts. This section illustrates the model's practical uses, highlighting how it's being integrated into industries and everyday tasks to enhance productivity, creativity, and learning.

Ethical and Societal Considerations

With great power comes great responsibility. This part addresses the ethical concerns surrounding the use of advanced language models like ChatGPT 4.0, including issues of misinformation, privacy, and the digital divide. It emphasizes the importance of responsible development and usage, as well as ongoing efforts to mitigate potential harms.

Chapter 9: Superintelligence and Beyond

Chapters 8 and 9 bridge the gap between current applications of AI, represented by technologies like ChatGPT 4.0, and future possibilities, including the advent of superintelligence. By providing a balanced overview of both the potentials and challenges, these chapters aim to equip readers with a comprehensive understanding of AI's trajectory and its implications for society.

To round off our exploration into the vast and dynamic realm of artificial intelligence, let's delve into the themes of governance, societal preparedness, and the proactive steps individuals and communities can take towards a future integrated with AI. These last three chapters will cover "AI in Governance and Society," "Preparing for an AI Future," and "Embracing AI: A Call to Action."

The Path to Superintelligence

Superintelligence refers to an AI that surpasses human intelligence in all aspects, from creativity and emotional intelligence to general wisdom and problem-solving abilities. This chapter outlines the theoretical pathways to achieving superintelligence, including the challenges and milestones along the way.

Potential Impacts and Scenarios

The possibility of super intelligent AI raises profound questions about the future of humanity. This section explores various scenarios, both optimistic and cautionary, detailing how superintelligence could revolutionize society, technology, and our understanding of intelligence itself. It also discusses the existential risks and ethical dilemmas posed by such advanced AI.

Navigating the Risks

Addressing the risks associated with superintelligence is crucial for ensuring a beneficial outcome for humanity. This part of the chapter delves into the strategies for risk mitigation, including AI alignment, containment protocols, and international collaboration on AI safety standards and governance.

Envisioning a Coexistent Future

The final section reflects on the prospects of coexisting with super intelligent AI, emphasizing the importance of proactive planning, ethical considerations, and fostering a symbiotic relationship between humans and AI. It invites readers to consider how society can prepare for and shape a future that includes super intelligent beings.

Chapter 10: AI in Governance and Society

This chapter examines the crucial role of governance in harnessing AI's potential for societal benefit while mitigating its risks. It explores the development of AI policies and frameworks that prioritize ethical considerations, accountability, and inclusivity.

The Path to Superintelligence

Superintelligence refers to an AI that surpasses human intelligence in all aspects, from creativity and emotional intelligence to general wisdom and problem-solving abilities. This chapter outlines the theoretical pathways to achieving superintelligence, including the challenges and milestones along the way.

Potential Impacts and Scenarios

The possibility of super intelligent AI raises profound questions about the future of humanity. This section explores various scenarios, both optimistic and cautionary, detailing how superintelligence could revolutionize society, technology, and our understanding of intelligence itself. It also discusses the existential risks and ethical dilemmas posed by such advanced AI.

Navigating the Risks

Addressing the risks associated with superintelligence is crucial for ensuring a beneficial outcome for humanity. This part of the chapter delves into the strategies for risk mitigation, including AI alignment, containment protocols, and international collaboration on AI safety standards and governance.

Envisioning a Coexistent Future

The final section reflects on the prospects of coexisting with super intelligent AI, emphasizing the importance of proactive planning, ethical considerations, and fostering a symbiotic relationship between humans and AI. It invites readers to consider how society can prepare for and shape a future that includes super intelligent beings.

Governing AI for the Common Good

AI and Public Policy

Delve into how AI influences public policy decisions and the importance of transparent, informed policy-making processes that engage multiple stakeholders. The chapter highlights case studies where AI has been effectively integrated into public services, enhancing efficiency, accessibility, and citizen engagement.

Ethical Governance and Surveillance

A critical analysis of the balance between using AI for societal security and the risks of surveillance overreach. This section emphasizes ethical governance models that respect privacy rights and foster trust between citizens and institutions.

The Future of Democratic Participation

Concluding with a forward-looking perspective, this chapter discusses the potential of AI to revitalize democratic processes, from voting systems and public consultations to policy formulation, encouraging broader participation and more responsive governance.

Chapter 11: Preparing for an AI Future

This chapter underscores the importance of education and lifelong learning as foundational elements in preparing for an AI-driven future. It discusses strategies for adapting educational systems to cultivate the skills necessary for thriving in a world augmented by AI technologies.

Lifelong Learning in the Age of AI

In an era where Artificial Intelligence (AI) is rapidly transforming industries, education, and lifelong learning stand as pivotal elements in equipping individuals for the future. The integration of AI technologies into various sectors is not just altering the landscape of employment but is also reshaping the skills required to thrive in the workforce.

The notion of lifelong learning—continuous, self-motivated pursuit of knowledge—has become more relevant than ever. In response, educational systems must evolve to cultivate not only technical skills related to AI and digital literacy but also soft skills such as creativity, critical thinking, and emotional intelligence. These competencies enable individuals to complement AI technologies rather than compete with them, fostering a workforce adept at leveraging AI for innovation and problem-solving.

As AI and automation become more prevalent, the workforce of tomorrow will witness a significant shift. Traditional job roles may evolve or disappear, while new categories of employment will emerge, reflecting the symbiosis between human ingenuity and AI capabilities. For instance, roles in AI ethics, machine learning model management, and data privacy are becoming increasingly important.

Organizations and individuals alike face the challenge of navigating this transition. Adapting to these changes requires a proactive approach to skill development, with an emphasis on continuous learning and flexibility. Employers play a crucial role in facilitating this transition, offering training programs and opportunities for skill enhancement that align with the shifting demands of the AI-augmented workplace.

Policy Recommendations for a Sustainable AI Future

To ensure a sustainable integration of AI into society, comprehensive policy recommendations are essential. These policies should encompass a range of objectives, including:

- **Investment in AI Literacy:** Governments and educational institutions should prioritize AI literacy, ensuring that individuals from diverse backgrounds have access to the knowledge and tools necessary to understand and engage with AI technologies. This includes basic education on AI's principles and its societal implications, aiming to demystify the technology and promote an informed public discourse.

- **Ethical Research and Development Practices:** Ethical considerations should be at the forefront of AI research and development. This involves creating guidelines that encourage transparency, accountability, and fairness in AI systems, addressing issues such as bias, privacy, and security. Encouraging ethical innovation can help mitigate potential harms and foster public trust in AI technologies.

- **Frameworks for International Cooperation on AI Standards and Safety:** Given the global impact of AI, international cooperation is vital in establishing standards and safety protocols. This entails collaborative efforts to define ethical guidelines, share best practices, and ensure that AI development aligns with shared human values. By working together, nations can leverage AI's potential while minimizing risks associated with its deployment.

Conclusion

Preparing for an AI future is a multifaceted endeavour that requires collective action from educators, policymakers, organizations, and individuals. By embracing education and lifelong learning, adapting to the evolving workforce, and implementing forward-thinking policies, society can navigate the challenges and opportunities presented by AI. This preparation will not only enable individuals to thrive in an AI-augmented world but also ensure that the development and integration of AI technologies contribute positively to the common good, fostering a sustainable and inclusive future.

Chapter 12: Embracing AI: A Call to Action

Addressing common fears and misconceptions about AI, this chapter aims to demystify the technology, encouraging a balanced understanding of its capabilities and limitations. It advocates for an informed and rational approach to the opportunities and challenges presented by AI.

Overcoming AI Anxiety

The emergence of Artificial Intelligence (AI) has sparked a revolution across various sectors, from healthcare to finance, enhancing efficiency and opening new possibilities. However, this rapid advancement has also led to a sense of apprehension among the public, often fuelled by misconceptions and sensationalized media portrayals. This fear, known as AI anxiety, stems from concerns over job displacement, loss of privacy, and the ethical implications of autonomous systems.

To mitigate these fears, it's crucial to understand AI's limitations and the ethical frameworks guiding its development. AI operates within the constraints set by its creators and is far from the sentient beings often depicted in science fiction. By fostering an informed understanding of how AI works and its potential benefits, we can alleviate undue fear and encourage a more rational perspective on its integration into society.

Public Engagement and AI Literacy

Engaging the public in conversations about AI and increasing AI literacy are essential steps towards a society that harnesses AI for the greater good. Knowledge about AI shouldn't be confined to experts and technologists; rather, it should be accessible to everyone, enabling informed discussions about its application and governance.

To achieve this, educational initiatives that demystify AI and its applications are necessary. Workshops, open courses, and online platforms can serve as avenues for the public to gain a foundational understanding of AI. Moreover, involving diverse voices in the conversation ensures that the development and deployment of AI technologies reflect a broad spectrum of societal values and needs.

Visioning a Collaborative Future

The future of AI and humanity is not a zero-sum game; rather, it is a collaborative endeavour where both can thrive. Envisioning this future requires recognizing AI's role as a tool that, when used ethically, can augment human capabilities, address pressing global challenges, and enhance the quality of life for all.

This collaborative future depends on inclusive policies that ensure the benefits of AI are widely distributed and accessible. It also relies on continuous dialogue between AI developers, policymakers, and the public to navigate the ethical dilemmas and societal impacts of AI technologies. By working together, we can create an empowered society where AI serves as a catalyst for positive change, fostering innovation and inclusivity.

Conclusion

Embracing AI demands an informed and proactive approach. Overcoming AI anxiety, promoting public engagement and AI literacy, and envisioning a collaborative future are key steps towards integrating AI into society in a manner that respects ethical boundaries and maximizes its benefits. By addressing the challenges head-on and leveraging the opportunities AI presents, we can steer the development of AI towards a future that reflects our shared values and aspirations. This journey requires the collective effort of all stakeholders to ensure that AI serves as a force for good, enhancing human lives and shaping a better future for generations to come.

Conclusions

Conclusions: Navigating the AI Horizon

These concluding chapters weave together the threads of understanding, preparation, and proactive engagement with AI, painting a picture of a future where AI is integrated into the fabric of society in a way that enhances human capabilities, upholds ethical standards, and fosters inclusivity. By empowering readers with knowledge and a call to action, the book aims to contribute to a global dialogue on shaping the role of AI in our collective future.

Crafting a conclusion for a comprehensive exploration into artificial intelligence, as outlined in the previous chapters, involves summarizing the key insights, reflecting on the journey of understanding AI, and looking forward to the role AI is poised to play in our future. Let's encapsulate the essence of this exploration in a manner that resonates with readers from all walks

As we stand at the precipice of a future interwoven with artificial intelligence, it's imperative to reflect on the journey we've embarked upon through the pages of this book. We've traversed the landscape of AI, from its fundamental principles and technological underpinnings to its societal impacts and ethical considerations. Along the way, we've demystified complex concepts, illuminated the transformative power of AI in various domains, and grappled with the moral and philosophical questions that arise as we forge ahead into an AI-augmented era. This concluding chapter seeks to distill the essence of our exploration, offering reflections, insights, and a visionary outlook for the role of AI in shaping our collective future.

Reflecting on the AI Journey

Our journey began with a dive into the history and evolution of AI, understanding its roots and the exponential trajectory of its development. We uncovered the mechanisms that drive AI systems, from neural networks to algorithms, and how these technologies empower machines to learn, reason, and interact in increasingly sophisticated ways. Through real-world applications, we witnessed AI's pervasive influence on our daily lives, transforming industries, enhancing productivity, and redefining possibilities.

As we ventured deeper, we encountered the ethical landscape that surrounds AI, confronting the challenges of bias, privacy, and accountability. The narrative then shifted to the alignment of AI with human values, a crucial endeavour to ensure that as AI systems grow in capability, they remain tethered to the principles that uphold the dignity and rights of all individuals.

The exploration of ChatGPT 4.0 and the concept of superintelligence broadened our perspective on what AI can achieve and the future scenarios we might face. These discussions not only highlighted the potential for AI to exceed human intelligence but also underscored the importance of governance, preparation, and ethical foresight in navigating the uncertainties of such advancements.

Key Insights and Takeaways

From this comprehensive exploration, several key insights emerge:

- AI as a Mirror and a Catalyst: AI reflects our desires to understand intelligence and enhance human capabilities. It also acts as a catalyst for societal transformation, pushing the boundaries of what is possible.

- The Dual-Edged Sword of Technology: AI's potential to benefit society is immense, yet it carries inherent risks and ethical dilemmas that demand vigilant oversight and responsible stewardship.

- The Imperative of Inclusivity and Ethics: Ensuring the benefits of AI are broadly shared and its development is guided by ethical principles is paramount. This includes addressing bias, ensuring transparency, and fostering equitable access to AI technologies.

- A Future Shaped by Collaboration: The trajectory of AI will be determined by the collective efforts of policymakers, technologists, ethicists, and the public. Engaging in open, informed dialogue and cooperation is essential for crafting a future where AI serves the common good.

Looking Forward: The Role of AI in Our Future

As we look to the horizon, the role of AI in our future is both promising and uncertain. What is clear, however, is the transformative impact AI is poised to have on every facet of our lives. From augmenting human capabilities and addressing global challenges to reshaping the landscapes of work, creativity, and social interaction, AI offers unparalleled opportunities for advancement and enrichment.

Yet, as we chart this course, it is crucial to navigate with caution, wisdom, and a deep commitment to ethical values. The future of AI is not predestined but will be shaped by the choices we make today. It is incumbent upon us to foster an AI future that amplifies human dignity, promotes societal well-being, and safeguards against the erosion of fundamental rights and freedoms.

A Call to Action

In closing, this journey through the world of AI is not merely an academic or technological exploration but a call to action. It invites each of us to engage with AI, not as passive observers but as active participants in shaping its role in our world. Whether through advocating for ethical AI practices, educating ourselves and others, or contributing to the development of responsible AI technologies, we all have a role to play.

The future of AI offers a canvas of boundless possibilities. Together, let's embrace the challenge of painting a future that reflects our highest aspirations, grounded in the principles of inclusivity, ethics, and human-centric technology. As we stand on the brink of this new era, let us move forward with hope, determination, and a shared vision for a world enhanced, not overshadowed, by artificial intelligence.

This conclusion aims to encapsulate the journey through the multifaceted world of AI, offering a reflective summary and a forward-looking perspective. It emphasizes the collective responsibility and opportunity to steer.

PART II

The 21 Frequently Asked Questions for Beginners to AI

Frequently Asked Questions (FAQs) tailored for beginners in the AI field is a great way to engage and educate ourselves. Here's a list of 21 FAQs that cover a broad spectrum of beginner interests and concerns, ranging from foundational concepts to ethical considerations. This list is designed to be accessible and intriguing for non-technical readers:

This selection covers a broad range of topics that are frequently queried by AI novices, ensuring that readers gain a well-rounded understanding of AI's capabilities, its societal impacts, and the ethical considerations it raises. These questions aim to demystify AI technology, discuss its practical applications, and address common concerns and misconceptions.

1. What is Artificial Intelligence (AI)?

2. How does AI differ from human intelligence?

3. What are the main types of AI, and how do they vary?

4. How do machines learn in AI?

5. What is Chat GPT, and how does it work?

6. Can AI make decisions on its own?

7. What is the role of data in AI?

8. How is AI used in everyday life?

9. What are the ethical considerations with AI?

10. Is AI going to replace human jobs?

11. How can AI be biased, and what are the implications?

12. What is the importance of AI in healthcare?

13. How can AI impact education?

14. What are the environmental impacts of AI?

15. How secure is AI from hackers?

16. Can AI create art or music?

17. How does AI affect privacy?

18. What is the future of AI?

19. How can someone start learning about AI?

20. What are the limitations of AI?

21. How can we ensure AI is used for the benefit of society?

Short Answers To The 21 Faqs

Let's dive into providing informative, engaging, and inspiring answers to these FAQs, aimed at non-technical readers interested in the world of Artificial Intelligence (AI).

This concise overview provides a starting point for readers who have questions and need answers to understand the fascinating world of AI, its capabilities, challenges, and the ethical considerations that accompany its development and application.

Q1. What is Artificial Intelligence (AI)?

Artificial Intelligence (AI) is a branch of computer science focused on creating machines capable of performing tasks that typically require human intelligence. This includes problem-solving, recognizing speech, translating languages, and more. AI systems can learn from experience, adapt to new inputs, and perform human-like tasks with increasing accuracy.

Q2. How does AI differ from human intelligence?

While human intelligence involves consciousness, emotions, and cognitive abilities developed through experiences and learning, AI simulates these cognitive functions through algorithms and computational power. Unlike humans, AI lacks consciousness and emotional understanding but can process and analyse large amounts of data at incredible speeds.

Q3. What are the main types of AI, and how do they vary

There are primarily three types of AI: Narrow or Weak AI, designed to perform specific tasks; General AI, which has the understanding and cognitive abilities of a human being; and Super Intelligent AI, which surpasses human intelligence. Currently, most AI applications are Narrow AI, excelling in particular tasks but without broader understanding or consciousness.

Q4. How do machines learn in AI?

Machines learn in AI through a process called machine learning, where algorithms analyse and learn from data to make decisions or predictions. Over time, as the system is exposed to more data, its ability to make accurate predictions or decisions improves, simulating a form of learning.

Q5. What is ChatGPT, and how does it work?

ChatGPT is an advanced AI model developed by Open AI, designed to understand, and generate human-like text based on the input it receives. It's trained on a vast dataset of text from the internet, allowing it to respond to queries, simulate conversation, and even create content that feels natural and human-like.

Q6. Can AI make decisions on its own?

AI can make decisions based on its programming and the data it processes. However, these decisions are ultimately guided by the objectives, constraints, and logic defined by humans. In this sense, AI doesn't possess free will but can autonomously analyse data and provide recommendations or take actions within its defined scope.

Q7. What is the role of data in AI?

Data is crucial in AI as it serves as the foundation for learning and decision-making. The quality, diversity, and volume of data directly impact the AI's performance. Through analysing data, AI models can identify patterns, make predictions, and improve their accuracy over time.

Q8. How is AI used in everyday life?

AI is increasingly integrated into our daily lives, from voice assistants on our smartphones, recommendation systems on streaming platforms, to navigation and traffic predictions in maps. It enhances user experiences, increases efficiency, and helps in making informed decisions.

Q9. What are the ethical considerations with AI?

Ethical considerations include concerns about privacy, surveillance, job displacement, and the fairness of AI systems. Ensuring AI is developed and used in a way that is equitable, transparent, and respects privacy is vital for its positive societal impact.

Q10. Is AI going to replace human jobs?

While AI will automate some tasks, it also creates new job opportunities and demands for skills in AI management, development, and ethics. The focus is shifting towards AI complementing human abilities, enhancing productivity, and fostering creativity.

Q11. How can AI be biased, and what are the implications?

AI systems can inherit biases from the data they are trained on, leading to unfair or discriminatory outcomes. Addressing bias involves carefully curating datasets, designing algorithms responsibly, and continuously monitoring and adjusting AI systems.

Q12. What is the importance of AI in healthcare?

AI plays a crucial role in healthcare by improving diagnostic accuracy, personalizing treatment plans, and managing patient data. It can analyze vast datasets to identify patterns and predictions that humans might miss, leading to better patient outcomes.

Q13. How can AI impact education?

AI can personalize learning experiences, provide real-time feedback, and automate administrative tasks, allowing educators to focus on teaching. It offers students tailored learning resources, adapting to their pace and style of learning.

Q14. What are the environmental impacts of AI?

The training and operation of large AI models require significant computational resources and energy, contributing to carbon emissions. However, AI also offers solutions for monitoring and reducing environmental impacts through efficient energy use, predicting climate patterns, and aiding in conservation efforts.

Q15. How secure is AI from hackers?

Like any technology, AI systems can be vulnerable to cyber-attacks. Ensuring AI security involves robust encryption, constant monitoring, and incorporating security by design principles. Addressing these vulnerabilities is critical for maintaining trust and integrity in AI applications.

Q16. Can AI create art or music?

Yes, AI can generate art, music, and other forms of creative content. By learning from existing works, AI algorithms can produce new creations that are unique and sometimes indistinguishable from human-made art. However, the creativity and emotional depth perceived in AI-generated art often spark discussions about the nature of creativity and the role of human experience in art.

Q17. How does AI affect privacy?

AI can process vast amounts of personal data, raising concerns about privacy and surveillance. Ensuring that AI respects privacy involves implementing strict data handling policies, transparency in AI operations, and giving individuals control over their data.

Q18. What is the future of AI?

The future of AI promises even greater integration into society, improving efficiencies, creating new industries, and solving complex problems. However, this future also requires careful consideration of ethical, social, and economic implications to ensure technology benefits all of humanity.

Q19. How can someone start learning about AI?

Starting with online courses, tutorials, and books targeted at beginners is a good approach. Many resources introduce AI concepts without requiring a deep technical background. Engaging with communities and practicing through projects can also enhance understanding and skills.

Q20. What are the limitations of AI?

AI's limitations include challenges in understanding context, the need for large datasets for training, vulnerability to biased data, and the lack of emotional intelligence. Addressing these limitations requires ongoing research and development.

Q21. How can we ensure AI is used for the benefit of society?

Ensuring AI benefits society involves developing and enforcing ethical guidelines, promoting transparency and accountability, engaging diverse stakeholders in AI governance, and focusing on applications that address societal challenges.

More Comprehensive Answers to The 21 Faqs

Creating detailed, comprehensive answers for each of the 21 questions, would provide a robust foundation and varied examples across different topics. This approach will help to ensure quality and greater depth in the information provided.

Q1. What is Artificial Intelligence (AI)?

Artificial Intelligence (AI), at its essence, represents a frontier of computer science dedicated to creating systems capable of performing tasks that would traditionally require human intelligence. These tasks range from recognizing speech and making decisions to translating languages and identifying patterns within large sets of data. The pursuit of AI is not merely about automating routine tasks but about augmenting human capabilities and tackling complex problems with unprecedented efficiency and scale.

The Genesis and Evolution of AI

The concept of AI dates back to ancient myths and stories of artificial beings endowed with intelligence or consciousness by master craftsmen. However, the formal foundation of AI as a scientific discipline began in the mid-20th century, rooted in the proposal that human intelligence can be so precisely described that a machine can be made to simulate it. This journey saw the development of algorithms that enabled computers to solve mathematical problems, play games like chess, and eventually, understand human languages.

AI has evolved through various stages, from the creation of basic algorithms and rule-based systems that mimic logical reasoning, to the development of machine learning (ML) and deep learning models that learn from data. Today's AI systems, powered by advanced neural networks, can analyse complex data, recognize patterns, and make predictions with a degree of accuracy that was previously unattainable.

Real-World Applications of AI

AI's applications are as diverse as its potential. In healthcare, AI algorithms assist in diagnosing diseases, predicting patient outcomes, and personalizing treatment plans. In finance, AI is used for fraud detection, risk management, and automated trading. The automotive industry employs AI in the development of self-driving cars, enhancing safety and efficiency on the roads.

One of the most visible applications of AI in daily life is in consumer technology, such as smart assistants (e.g., Siri, Alexa) that can understand and respond to natural language queries, making technology more accessible and intuitive. In the realm of entertainment, AI algorithms personalize content recommendations on platforms like Netflix and Spotify, transforming how people discover movies, TV shows, and music.

Challenges and Ethical Considerations

As AI becomes more integrated into society, it raises significant ethical, social, and economic challenges. One of the most pressing concerns is the potential for AI to exacerbate inequality and bias. Since AI systems learn from data, they can perpetuate and amplify biases present in that data, leading to unfair outcomes. Ensuring that AI is developed and deployed in an equitable and ethical manner requires rigorous oversight, transparency, and collaboration across sectors.

Another concern is the impact of AI on employment. While AI can automate routine tasks, potentially displacing certain jobs, it also creates new opportunities for jobs that require AI oversight, ethical considerations, and the development of new technologies. The future of work with AI will likely emphasize the augmentation of human abilities rather than outright replacement.

Looking Forward

The future of AI promises even greater advances, with potential breakthroughs in fields such as quantum computing, which could exponentially increase AI's processing power. As AI continues to evolve, it holds the promise of solving some of humanity's most pressing challenges, from combating climate change to advancing medical research. However, realizing AI's full potential will require careful stewardship to ensure that the benefits of AI technologies are accessible to all and that their development is guided by ethical principles.

This expansion offers a glimpse into the breadth and depth of AI, illustrating its foundational concepts, real-world applications, and the challenges and ethical considerations it presents.

Given the depth and length required for each answer, I'll begin with a detailed response to the first question. This approach will allow me to provide a comprehensive and nuanced exploration of how AI differs from human intelligence.

Q2: How does AI differ from human intelligence?

Artificial Intelligence (AI) and human intelligence embody the convergence of computational prowess and the essence of human cognition, respectively. While both AI and human intelligence can perform tasks, solve problems, and make decisions, the underlying mechanisms, capabilities, and limitations of each are fundamentally distinct. Understanding these differences not only sheds light on the nature of intelligence itself but also on the potential and challenges of AI as it becomes an integral part of our lives.

The Basis of Intelligence

Human intelligence is a complex trait that encompasses cognitive processes, emotional depth, and social interactions. It arises from the biological and neurological structures of the human brain, shaped by millions of years of evolution. Human cognition is characterized by its flexibility and adaptability, allowing individuals to learn from limited information, apply knowledge in diverse contexts, and exhibit creativity and emotional responses.

In contrast, AI is a product of computer science, designed to simulate aspects of human intelligence through algorithms and computational models. AI systems, particularly those based on machine learning, are trained on data sets to perform specific tasks, from recognizing speech to playing chess. However, AI lacks consciousness, self-awareness, and the emotional nuances inherent in human intelligence.

Learning and Adaptability

One of the most profound differences between AI and human intelligence lies in their learning processes and adaptability. Humans can learn from a few examples or even a single experience, drawing on intuition, abstract thinking, and a rich tapestry of prior knowledge. Human learning is deeply contextual, influenced by emotional and social factors, enabling a nuanced understanding of the world.

AI, particularly through machine learning and deep learning, learns from data. The more data an AI system is exposed to, the better it can perform its task. However, this learning is highly specific to the task at hand and requires vast amounts of data for accuracy. AI systems generally lack the ability to generalize knowledge across vastly different domains or to apply learned concepts in novel situations as fluidly as humans can.

Creativity & Emotional Intelligence

Creativity and emotional intelligence represent another area of divergence. Human creativity is not merely about generating something new but involves the ability to make connections between seemingly unrelated concepts, to think abstractly, and to imbue creations with emotional depth and cultural significance. Similarly, human emotional intelligence—the ability to perceive, use, understand, manage, and express emotions—plays a crucial role in decision-making, empathy, and social interactions.

AI has made strides in areas that mimic creativity, such as generating art, music, or writing. However, these processes are based on analyzing patterns in existing works and generating output based on statistical likelihoods. AI's "creativity" lacks the intentionality, emotional depth, and cultural context that human creativity possesses. Similarly, while AI can simulate aspects of emotional intelligence, such as recognizing human emotions through facial expressions or text, it does not experience emotions and thus cannot fully comprehend their complexity.

Ethical and Moral Reasoning

Ethical and moral reasoning is inherently human, rooted in cultural values, personal experiences, and social norms. Humans navigate ethical dilemmas using not only rational thought but also empathy and moral intuition. This aspect of human intelligence is challenging to replicate in AI, as ethical reasoning involves weighing multiple, often conflicting, values and principles in context-specific situations.

AI can be programmed to follow ethical guidelines or make decisions based on ethical principles encoded into its algorithms. However, these decisions are ultimately determined by how the programmers define ethical parameters and the data the AI is trained on. The subtleties of human ethics, which require understanding context, intention, and the nuances of human relationships, remain beyond AI's current capabilities.

Conclusion

While AI mimics certain aspects of human intelligence, the fundamental differences between AI and human intelligence—rooted in the biological, emotional, and social dimensions of human cognition—highlight the complementary nature of human and artificial minds. Understanding these differences is crucial as we integrate AI into society, leveraging its strengths to enhance human capabilities while acknowledging its limitations. As AI continues to evolve, the dialogue between the potential of AI and the unique qualities of human intelligence will shape the future of technology, society, and our understanding of what it means to be intelligent.

Q3. What are the main types of AI, and how do they vary?

The journey through the landscape of Artificial Intelligence (AI) reveals a spectrum of technologies, each with unique capabilities, purposes, and stages of development. Understanding the main types of AI not only demystifies the field but also highlights the diverse potential of these technologies. There are primarily three categories into which AI systems can be classified: Narrow AI, General AI, and Super intelligent AI. Each represents different levels of complexity, autonomy, and versatility.

Narrow AI (Artificial Narrow Intelligence, ANI)

Narrow AI, also known as Weak AI, is designed to perform a specific task or a set of closely related tasks. Unlike its more advanced counterparts, Narrow AI operates under a limited pre-defined range or set of contexts. It's the most common and currently deployed form of AI in the world today. Examples abound in our daily lives, from voice assistants like Siri and Alexa to recommendation systems on Netflix and Spotify.

In healthcare, Narrow AI powers diagnostic tools that analyse images, such as X-rays and MRIs, with precision surpassing human radiologists in some tasks. In finance, it's used for fraud detection, leveraging patterns in data to identify irregularities that could indicate fraudulent activities. Narrow AI is characterized by its reliance on machine learning algorithms to process data, identify patterns, and make decisions based on its programming. However, it lacks the ability to perform beyond its specified tasks or adapt to new, unrelated problems.

General AI (Artificial General Intelligence, AGI)

Artificial General Intelligence represents a theoretical leap from Narrow AI. AGI would possess the ability to understand, learn, and apply its intelligence across a broad range of tasks, mirroring the cognitive abilities of a human being. An AGI system could perform any intellectual task that a human can do, from writing a symphony to solving complex mathematical problems and beyond.

The development of AGI is a goal that researchers are still working towards, with significant challenges in creating an AI that can truly understand and replicate the nuances of human intelligence, including emotional intelligence, creativity, and the ability to understand context in a manner like humans. The advent of AGI would mark a pivotal moment in AI research, bridging the gap between machines and the general problem-solving capabilities of humans.

Super -intelligent AI

Beyond AGI lies the concept of Super-Intelligent AI — a form of artificial intelligence that surpasses the brightest and most gifted human minds in practically every field, including scientific creativity, general wisdom, and social skills. The notion of Superintelligence suggests an AI that can not only improve itself but also create better, more efficient versions of itself without human intervention.

The implications of Super-intelligent AI are profound and the subject of much ethical and philosophical debate. Concerns revolve around control, safety, and the alignment of super-intelligent AI's goals with human values and interests. The potential for Superintelligence to solve complex global challenges is enormous, yet it poses existential risks if not developed and managed with extreme caution.

Conclusion

The classification of AI into Narrow, General, and Super-intelligent AI provides a framework for understanding the progression and potential of AI technologies. Currently, the world operates predominantly within the realm of Narrow AI, benefiting from its specialized applications. The quest for AGI and eventually Super-intelligent AI continues, carrying the promise of ground-breaking advancements alongside profound ethical, societal, and existential questions. As AI evolves, the dialogue surrounding its development, deployment, and governance becomes increasingly important, ensuring that AI serves the betterment of humanity.

Q4: How do machines learn in AI?

Machine learning, a core component of artificial intelligence (AI), enables machines to learn from data, improve their performance, and make decisions without being explicitly programmed for every task. This process involves three primary types of learning: supervised learning, unsupervised learning, and reinforcement learning.

Supervised learning is the most common method, where machines learn from labelled datasets. This means the model is trained on a dataset that includes both the input data and the correct output. Over time, the model learns to make predictions or classifications based on new, unseen data. For example, a supervised learning algorithm could be trained to recognize photos of cats by being shown thousands of labelled images

Unsupervised learning, on the other hand, deals with unlabelled data. The algorithm tries to learn the underlying patterns and structure from such data without any explicit instructions on what to look for. This type is often used for clustering and association tasks, such as grouping customers with similar buying behaviours.

Reinforcement learning involves training models to make a sequence of decisions. The machine learns to achieve a goal in an uncertain, potentially complex environment. In reinforcement learning, an agent learns to choose actions that maximize some notion of cumulative reward through trial-and-error interactions with a dynamic environment. This approach has been used successfully in game-playing AI like AlphaGo.

Machines learn by adjusting their algorithms based on the feedback received during the training process, gradually improving accuracy. This learning process involves complex mathematical algorithms and requires significant computational power, especially for tasks involving large datasets and complex decision-making.

Q5: What is ChatGPT, and how does it work?

ChatGPT, developed by Open AI, represents a groundbreaking advancement in the field of artificial intelligence. It's a variant of the GPT (Generative Pre-trained Transformer) language model, designed to understand and generate human-like text based on the input it receives. This capability makes ChatGPT an exceptional tool for a wide range of applications, from conducting natural language conversations to generating written content and even coding.

The magic behind ChatGPT lies in its training process, which involves feeding the model a vast dataset of text from the internet. This training enables ChatGPT to learn patterns, nuances, and the complexities of human language. When you interact with ChatGPT, it doesn't search the web for answers; instead, it draws on its extensive training to generate responses that reflect a deep understanding of the topic.

One of the key technologies behind ChatGPT is transformer architecture, enabling the model to consider the context of each word and phrase it generates, resulting in coherent and contextually appropriate responses. Additionally, ChatGPT undergoes fine-tuning through reinforcement learning from human feedback, where human trainers guide the model towards more accurate and helpful outputs.

Artificial Intelligence has seamlessly integrated into our daily routines, often in ways we might not immediately recognize. In the realm of personal assistance, AI powers voice-activated assistants like Siri and Alexa, helping us with everything from setting alarms to answering questions. In entertainment, streaming services like Netflix use AI to analyse viewing habits and recommend shows and movies tailored to individual tastes.

AI also enhances user experiences through smart home devices, which learn from our behaviours to adjust lighting, heating, and even order groceries. Navigation apps like Google Maps analyse vast amounts of data to provide real-time traffic updates and route suggestions, optimizing our travel plans.

In the background, AI algorithms help detect fraudulent transactions on our bank accounts, filter spam from our emails, and even tailor the advertisements we see online based on our browsing history and preferences, showcasing the pervasive and often beneficial role of AI in our daily lives.

Q6 Can AI make decisions on its own?

AI can make decisions within the parameters set by its programming and the data it has been trained on. However, it's essential to understand that AI does not possess consciousness or independent will. Its decision-making capabilities are confined to the scope of its designed algorithms and the objectives it has been tasked with.

In a sense, AI can autonomously analyse data, identify patterns, and make predictions or recommendations based on its training. For instance, AI in autonomous vehicles makes real-time decisions about speed, direction, and route based on sensor data and pre-defined algorithms. Similarly, AI in finance can make decisions on stock trades by analysing market data and trends.

Despite these capabilities, AI's decisions are ultimately dependent on human-defined goals and boundaries. Ethical and practical safeguards are essential to ensure that AI's decision-making aligns with human values and interests. As AI technology evolves, the ongoing challenge for developers and regulators is to ensure that AI systems remain transparent, accountable, and under human oversight, particularly in critical applications affecting safety, privacy, and social welfare.

Q7: What is the role of data in AI?

Data is the lifeblood of artificial intelligence (AI). It fuels the learning processes that enable AI systems to recognize patterns, make decisions, and predict outcomes. The quality, quantity, and diversity of the data directly influence the performance and reliability of AI models.

In supervised learning, for example, data acts as a teacher, providing examples for the AI to learn from. The algorithm iterates over this data, adjusting its parameters to minimize errors in its predictions or classifications. This process requires large volumes of high-quality data to ensure the AI can generalize well to new, unseen data.

Unsupervised learning uses data to uncover hidden patterns or structures without pre-labelled answers, highlighting the importance of diverse and comprehensive datasets for discovering insightful correlations.

Data not only enables the initial training of AI models but also their continuous improvement. Through ongoing exposure to new data, AI systems can adapt to changes over time, refining their predictions and decisions.

However, the role of data in AI also presents challenges, such as ensuring data privacy, security, and mitigating biases that can lead to unfair or discriminatory AI outcomes. Addressing these challenges requires careful data management practices, ethical guidelines, and often, regulatory oversight to ensure that AI serves the public good while respecting individual rights.

Given the space constraints and the depth required for each answer, I'll proceed with an in-depth response to the first question for now. Afterward, we can explore the second question in similar detail.

Q8 How is AI used in everyday life?

Artificial Intelligence (AI) has seamlessly woven itself into the fabric of our daily lives, often in ways that go unnoticed by the average person. From the moment we wake up to when we go to sleep, AI influences a variety of activities and decisions, enhancing convenience, efficiency, and personalization. Understanding the breadth of AI's application in everyday life underscores its significance and the subtle ways it shapes our interactions with technology and each other.

Personal Assistants and Smart Home Devices

One of the most direct interactions people have with AI is through personal assistants like Siri, Alexa, and Google Assistant. These AI-driven technologies use natural language processing (NLP) to understand spoken commands and perform tasks such as setting alarms, answering questions, playing music, or providing weather updates. The intelligence of these systems lies in their ability to parse human language, learn from interactions, and deliver personalized responses.

Smart home devices, including thermostats, lights, and security cameras, employ AI to learn from our habits and preferences, automating home management to optimize comfort and energy efficiency. For instance, smart thermostats can adjust the temperature based on your routine and preferences, learning over time to provide the ideal environment while conserving energy.

Navigation and Transportation

AI significantly enhances the efficiency and safety of transportation systems. Navigation apps like Google Maps and Waze use AI to analyze traffic data in real-time, providing users with the fastest routes, traffic updates, and estimated arrival times. This capability is not just about convenience but also about reducing congestion and improving road safety.

In the realm of autonomous vehicles, AI is the cornerstone technology enabling cars to perceive their environment, make decisions, and navigate without human intervention. Through a combination of sensors, cameras, and advanced algorithms, self-driving cars can detect obstacles, interpret traffic signals, and adjust their actions, accordingly, promising a future of safer, more efficient transportation.

Online Shopping and Customer Service

AI transforms the online shopping experience by providing personalized recommendations based on browsing and purchase history. E-commerce platforms like Amazon use machine learning algorithms to analyse your interactions and preferences, suggesting products you might like, thereby making shopping more tailored and efficient.

In customer service, chatbots powered by AI handle inquiries and provide assistance 24/7. These bots can answer common questions, process orders, and escalate issues when necessary, improving service quality while reducing the workload on human staff.

Healthcare

AI's application in healthcare is revolutionizing diagnosis, treatment, and patient care. Machine learning algorithms can analyse medical images, such as X-rays and MRIs, with precision that matches or even surpasses human radiologists, aiding in the early detection of diseases like cancer. AI also plays a critical role in developing personalized medicine, where treatments are optimized based on an individual's genetic makeup, lifestyle, and other factors.

Entertainment and Media

Streaming services like Netflix and Spotify leverage AI to curate personalized content recommendations, ensuring users discover shows, movies, and music aligned with their tastes. This personalization extends to news aggregators and social media platforms, where AI algorithms filter and prioritize content, shaping the information and entertainment landscapes we navigate daily.

Financial Services

In finance, AI enhances security and customer service. Fraud detection algorithms analyse transaction patterns to identify and prevent unauthorized activity, protecting consumers and financial institutions alike. Robo-advisors provide personalized investment advice and portfolio management, making financial planning more accessible and tailored to individual goals.

Conclusion

The ubiquity of AI in everyday life highlights its transformative potential across various sectors. By automating routine tasks, enhancing decision-making, and personalizing experiences, AI not only increases efficiency but also opens up new possibilities for innovation and convenience. As AI technologies continue to evolve, their integration into daily life is set to deepen, making it essential to understand and engage with AI as an empowering tool for the future.

Q9: What are the ethical considerations with AI?

The integration of AI into various aspects of society raises profound ethical considerations. One of the primary concerns is privacy, as AI systems can collect and analyse personal data on an unprecedented scale. There's also the risk of bias, where AI algorithms may perpetuate or even amplify existing societal biases if they're trained on skewed or unrepresentative data.

Another ethical issue is the impact of AI on employment, with automation threatening to displace jobs in certain sectors. This shift calls for strategies to ensure the workforce can adapt, emphasizing retraining and education in AI-related fields.

Transparency and accountability in AI decision-making processes are crucial, particularly in high-stakes areas like criminal justice and healthcare. Ensuring that AI systems can be audited, and their decisions explained is vital for maintaining public trust and safeguarding individual rights.

Q10: Is AI going to replace human jobs?

The impact of AI on the job market is complex and multifaceted. While AI and automation can lead to the displacement of certain jobs, particularly those involving routine, repetitive tasks, they also create new opportunities in emerging fields and industries.

AI has the potential to automate tasks such as data entry, basic customer service inquiries, and simple diagnostic assessments, which could reduce the demand for jobs in these areas. However, this automation can also lead to increased efficiency, reduced errors, and potentially lower costs for consumers.

At the same time, the growth of AI is generating new jobs in AI development, management, ethics, and policy. There's also an increased need for roles that require human creativity, empathy, and interpersonal skills—areas where AI cannot easily replicate human performance.

The key to navigating the impact of AI on employment is adaptation and education. Investing in workforce retraining and education can help individuals transition to the new jobs created by the AI and technology sector. Additionally, policymakers and businesses need to consider the broader social and economic implications of AI-driven automation, ensuring that the benefits of AI are shared across society and support is provided to those affected by job displacement.

Q11: How can AI be biased, and what are the implications?

AI bias occurs when an AI system reflects the prejudices present in its training data or design, leading to unfair outcomes for certain groups of people. This can happen in various ways, such as through biased data sets that do not accurately represent the diversity of the real world, flawed algorithms that perpetuate existing disparities, or the misapplication of AI technologies.

For example, if an AI system used for hiring is trained on historical employment data that reflects gender or racial imbalances in certain roles, it may inadvertently favour candidates who fit the profiles of past hires, perpetuating existing inequalities.

The implications of AI bias can be significant, affecting everything from job opportunities to legal outcomes and healthcare decisions. Biased AI can reinforce social stereotypes and inequalities, undermine trust in AI technologies, and cause harm to individuals and communities.

Addressing AI bias requires a multi-pronged approach, including diversifying data sets, implementing algorithmic transparency and accountability, and involving diverse groups in AI development and decision-making processes. Ongoing monitoring and testing for bias, as well as the development of ethical guidelines and regulatory frameworks, are also crucial in mitigating the risks of biased AI.

Q12: What is the importance of AI in healthcare?

In healthcare, AI is revolutionizing diagnosis, treatment, and patient care, offering unprecedented opportunities to improve outcomes. AI algorithms can analyse medical images, such as X-rays and MRIs, with a level of precision and speed that supplements human expertise, aiding in early and accurate disease detection.

AI also enables personalized medicine, where treatments and medications are optimized for individual patients based on their unique genetic makeup and lifestyle, enhancing efficacy, and reducing side effects. Additionally, AI-powered tools can monitor patient vitals and predict deteriorations in health, enabling timely interventions even in remote care settings.

The importance of AI in healthcare extends to administrative tasks, reducing the burden on healthcare providers by automating paperwork, scheduling, and patient communication, allowing medical professionals to focus more on patient care.

Q13: How can AI impact education?

AI has the potential to transform education by personalizing learning, increasing accessibility, and automating administrative tasks, thus allowing educators to focus more on teaching and less on bureaucracy.

Personalized learning is one of the most promising applications of AI in education. AI systems can analyse a student's performance, learning style, and preferences to tailor educational content, suggest resources, and adjust difficulty levels in real-time. This can help address the diverse needs of students, making learning more engaging and effective for everyone.

AI can also increase accessibility in education, providing language translation, real-time captioning, and customized learning experiences for students with disabilities. Furthermore, AI-driven tutoring systems can offer additional support outside the classroom, helping students master concepts at their own pace.

On the administrative side, AI can automate tasks such as grading, scheduling, and tracking student progress, reducing the workload on teachers and allowing them to dedicate more time to student interaction and instruction.

However, the integration of AI in education also raises concerns about data privacy, the digital divide, and the need for human oversight in learning processes. Ensuring equitable access to AI-enhanced education and addressing these challenges will be critical to realizing AI's full potential in transforming educational experiences.

Q14: What are the environmental impacts of AI?

The environmental impact of AI is a growing concern, with implications for energy consumption, electronic waste, and the carbon footprint associated with training and running AI models.

Training complex AI models, especially deep learning systems, requires significant computational power, which in turn demands substantial electricity. This energy consumption can contribute to greenhouse gas emissions, particularly if the power comes from non-renewable sources. The operation of data centres, which host the servers running AI algorithms, further adds to the environmental impact, necessitating efficient cooling systems and energy usage.

However, AI also offers solutions to environmental challenges. AI can optimize energy consumption in buildings and transportation, reduce waste through smarter logistics and manufacturing processes, and enhance climate change models, helping scientists and policymakers make informed decisions.

Balancing the environmental costs and benefits of AI involves improving the energy efficiency of AI technologies, transitioning to renewable energy sources for power needs, and leveraging AI to tackle pressing environmental issues. Ongoing research and innovation are key to minimizing AI's environmental footprint while maximizing its potential to contribute to sustainable development.

Each of these topics opens a window into the multifaceted world of AI, shedding light on its capabilities, challenges, and the considerations necessary for its ethical and effective integration into society.

Q15 How secure is AI from hackers?

As AI systems become increasingly integral to our digital infrastructure, ensuring their security against hackers is paramount. AI systems, like any technology, are vulnerable to cyber threats. Hackers can exploit weaknesses in AI algorithms to manipulate outcomes, steal data, or even disable the AI systems entirely.

To counter these threats, developers incorporate robust security measures during the AI development process, including encryption, regular security audits, and employing AI itself to identify and respond to cyber threats more rapidly. However, as AI technologies evolve, so do the tactics of cybercriminals, necessitating constant vigilance and innovation in cybersecurity measures.

Ensuring the security of AI involves a comprehensive approach, including safeguarding the data used to train AI models, protecting the AI systems themselves, and continuously monitoring for and responding to threats. It's a dynamic challenge that requires collaboration across industries and disciplines to keep AI systems and the data they process secure from hackers.

Q16. Can AI create art or music?

The answer is a resounding yes. AI's capabilities in these domains have grown significantly, offering new tools for creative expression, and challenging ssssour understanding of creativity. While the debate about the value and authenticity of AI-generated art and music continues, what remains clear is that AI's role in the arts is not just a novelty but a burgeoning field that promises to reshape the creative landscape. As we navigate this new terrain, the dialogue between technology and creativity will be crucial in shaping a future where art and music continue to reflect the full breadth of human and artificial intelligence.

The question of whether AI can create art or music touches on the intersections of technology, creativity, and the essence of human expression. In recent years, the capabilities of AI in the fields of art and music have seen remarkable advancements, challenging traditional notions of creativity and the role of the artist. To explore this topic, we delve into how AI is being used to generate art and music, the implications of these developments, and the ongoing debate about creativity and authorship.

AI in Art Creation

AI's foray into the art world has been facilitated by algorithms known as Generative Adversarial Networks (GANs) and other machine learning models. These algorithms analyse vast datasets of artwork, learning styles, techniques, and the nuances that define different art movements. Once trained, they can generate new artworks that, to the untrained eye, might be indistinguishable from those created by human hands.

Projects like Google's Deep Dream and the artwork generated by GANs have showcased the ability of AI to produce visually compelling images. These pieces often carry a surreal, dream-like quality, revealing patterns and possibilities that might not occur to human artists. The AI-generated portrait "Edmond de Bellamy," which sold at auction for a significant sum, highlights the market's growing acceptance of AI-created art.

AI in Music Composition

In music, AI systems have been developed to compose pieces in various genres, from classical to pop and jazz. These systems analyse large collections of music to understand chord progressions, rhythms, and structures that define different styles. By processing this information, AI can then create new compositions that resonate with human listeners.

Tools like IBM's Watson Beat, Google's Magenta, and Open Ai's Jukebox demonstrate the potential for AI in music creation. These platforms allow users to input themes, moods, or even specific melodies, around which AI can craft complete compositions. The results have been diverse, ranging from entirely original pieces to works that mimic the styles of specific composers or artists.

Implications and Challenges

The ability of AI to create art and music raises profound questions about creativity, authorship, and the value of art. On one hand, AI-generated art and music can democratize creativity, providing tools for individuals without formal training to express themselves and explore new forms of artistic expression. It can also inspire human artists and musicians by suggesting novel ideas and collaborations between humans and AI, leading to unprecedented forms of art and music.

However, the rise of AI in creative domains also challenges the traditional concept of art as a uniquely human endeavour, deeply intertwined with the artist's experiences, emotions, and intentions. Critics argue that art created by AI lacks the depth and emotional resonance that come from human experiences, reducing art to mere aesthetics or technical skill.

Additionally, there are concerns about copyright and ownership. When an AI generates art or music, who is the creator? The programmer who designed the algorithm? The AI itself? Or perhaps the individual who provided the initial input or concept? These questions highlight the legal and ethical complexities surrounding AI-generated content.

The Future of AI in Creativity

Looking ahead, the role of AI in art and music is set to evolve further. As algorithms become more sophisticated and capable of understanding and replicating the subtleties of human creativity, the line between AI-generated and human-created works may blur even more. This evolution will likely prompt continued debate about the nature of creativity and the role of technology in the arts.

Moreover, as AI becomes more integrated into creative processes, the potential for collaborative works where humans and AI co-create could redefine artistic and musical expression. These collaborations can push the boundaries of creativity, leading to new art forms and experiences that were previously unimaginable.

Conclusion

Can AI create art or music? The answer is a resounding yes. AI's capabilities in these domains have grown significantly, offering new tools for creative expression, and challenging our understanding of creativity. While the debate about the value and authenticity of AI-generated art and music continues, what remains clear is that AI's role in the arts is not just a novelty but a burgeoning field that promises to reshape the creative landscape. As we navigate this new terrain, the dialogue between technology and creativity will be crucial in shaping a future where art and music continue to reflect the full breadth of human and artificial intelligence.

Q17: How does AI affect privacy?

In the digital age, AI has become a cornerstone of innovation, driving advancements across various sectors. However, its integration into our daily lives raises significant privacy concerns. AI systems, particularly those involving data analysis and facial recognition, have the capability to process vast amounts of personal information, leading to potential breaches of privacy.

The use of AI in social media algorithms, for instance, can reveal personal preferences and behaviours, which are then used to tailor advertisements or content, sometimes without explicit consent. Similarly, facial recognition technologies employed for security or surveillance purposes may track individuals without their knowledge, compiling data that could be misused.

Moreover, AI-driven data analysis can inadvertently expose sensitive information. AI algorithms can identify patterns and connections in data sets that were not previously apparent, potentially uncovering personal details that were meant to be anonymized.

To mitigate these risks, there's a growing call for robust data protection regulations and ethical AI development practices. Implementing stringent data handling procedures, ensuring transparency in how AI systems use data, and giving individuals control over their personal information are pivotal steps toward safeguarding privacy in the AI era.

Q18: What is the future of AI?

The future of AI holds both immense promise and challenges. As AI technologies evolve, we anticipate breakthroughs that could fundamentally transform healthcare, education, environmental conservation, and more. The development of AI could lead to more accurate medical diagnoses, personalized education plans, efficient energy use, and innovative solutions to climate change.

However, the trajectory of AI also depends on navigating ethical considerations, such as job displacement, privacy concerns, and the digital divide. Ensuring that AI benefits all sectors of society requires inclusive and equitable development strategies, focusing on ethical AI use and addressing potential negative impacts.

Looking ahead, the future of AI will likely see more collaborative human-AI interactions, where AI augments human capabilities rather than replaces them. With continued research, ethical oversight, and public engagement, AI has the potential to address some of the most pressing challenges facing humanity today.

Q19: How can someone start learning about AI?

Diving into AI might seem daunting, but with the plethora of resources available today, anyone can begin to unravel the mysteries of artificial intelligence. For beginners, online courses offer a structured path through the basics of AI, covering fundamental concepts and practical applications. Websites like Coursera, edX, and Udacity provide courses developed by universities and leading tech companies.

Books on AI for non-technical readers can also offer insights into the implications of AI for society and ethical considerations, alongside technical knowledge. Additionally, engaging with AI communities on platforms like Reddit or GitHub can provide support and insights from experienced individuals in the field.

Starting with projects, even simple ones, can demystify AI concepts and demonstrate their practical applications. Tools like TensorFlow and open-source datasets allow beginners to experiment with machine learning models and learn by doing.

Q20: What are the limitations of AI?

Despite its advances, AI faces several limitations. One significant challenge is the dependency on data quality and quantity. AI systems learn from data, meaning biased or insufficient datasets can lead to inaccurate or unfair outcomes. Additionally, AI struggles with tasks requiring common sense, creativity, and emotional intelligence, areas where human judgment still surpasses AI capabilities.

Another limitation is the explainability of AI decisions. Explainability (also referred to as "interpretability") is the concept that a machine learning model and its output can be explained in a way that "makes sense" to a human being at an acceptable level. Some AI models, particularly deep learning, act as "black boxes," where the decision-making process is not transparent, making it difficult to understand or trust their outcomes fully.

Addressing these limitations requires ongoing research, development of more sophisticated AI models, and ethical guidelines to ensure AI's responsible use and development.

Q21: How can we ensure AI is used for the benefit of society?

Ensuring AI benefits society involves a multi-faceted approach. Developing ethical guidelines for AI research and deployment is crucial, focusing on fairness, transparency, and accountability. Engaging diverse stakeholders in the development process can help identify potential negative impacts and societal needs, guiding more inclusive and equitable AI solutions.

Education and awareness are key to empowering individuals to understand and engage with AI technologies critically. Additionally, fostering collaboration between policymakers, researchers, and industry leaders can facilitate the development of regulations that promote ethical AI use and mitigate risks.

By prioritizing these approaches, we can steer AI development toward outcomes that enhance societal well-being and address global challenges, ensuring the technology serves as a force for good.

Glossary of AI Technology

Creating an exhaustive glossary of AI terminology is quite an endeavour, but I wish get beginners started with a selection of key terms that are fundamental to the field of AI. This list is designed to serve as a useful reference for beginners, covering a range of concepts from general AI theory to more specific technologies and methodologies. Keep in mind, the field of AI is vast and continually evolving, so this list cannot cover every term but will provide a solid foundation.

1. AI (Artificial Intelligence): The simulation of human intelligence in machines that are programmed to think like humans and mimic their actions. The term may also apply to any machine that exhibits traits associated with a human mind such as learning and problem-solving.

2. Machine Learning (ML): A subset of AI that includes algorithms and statistical models that computer systems use to perform a specific task without using explicit instructions, relying on patterns and inference instead.

3. Deep Learning: A subset of ML that involves neural networks with many layers. It's particularly powerful in tasks such as image and speech recognition.

4. Neural Network: A network or circuit of neurons, or in a modern sense, an artificial neural network composed of artificial neurons or nodes. It is used for machine learning and deep learning applications.

5. Supervised Learning: A type of machine learning where the model is trained on a labelled dataset, which means that each training example is paired with the output label.

6. Unsupervised Learning: A type of machine learning where the model is trained on a dataset without explicit instructions on what to do with it. The system tries to learn the patterns and the structure from the data.

7. Reinforcement Learning: A type of machine learning where an agent learns to behave in an environment by performing actions and seeing the results.

8. Natural Language Processing (NLP): A field of AI that gives the machines the ability to read, understand, and derive meaning from human languages.

9. Computer Vision: A field of AI that trains computers to interpret and understand the visual world. Machines can accurately identify and classify objects—and then react to what they "see" through cameras, videos, and deep learning models.

10. Algorithm: A set of rules to be followed in calculations or other problem-solving operations, especially by a computer.

11. TensorFlow: An open-source software library for dataflow and differentiable programming across a range of tasks, used for machine learning and deep learning applications.

12. PyTorch: An open-source machine learning library based on the Torch library, used for applications such as computer vision and natural language processing.

13. GAN (Generative Adversarial Network): A class of machine learning frameworks designed by two neural networks contesting with each other in a game.

14. Data Mining: The process of discovering patterns in large data sets involving methods at the intersection of machine learning, statistics, and database systems.

15. Bias: A systematic error introduced by an algorithm that affects the fairness of its outcomes.

16. Ethics in AI: The branch of ethics that examines the moral aspects of technology use and the development of algorithms, including issues of fairness, transparency, accountability, and privacy.

17. Robotics: A field related to AI, focusing on the design, construction, operation, and use of robots.

18. Big Data: Extremely large data sets that may be analysed computationally to reveal patterns, trends, and associations, especially relating to human behaviour and interactions.

19. Cloud Computing: The delivery of different services through the Internet, including data storage, servers, databases, networking, and software.

20. IoT (Internet of Things): The network of physical objects—devices, vehicles, appliances—that are embedded with sensors, software, and other technologies for the purpose of connecting and exchanging data with other devices and systems over the Internet.

21. Explainability of AI Decisions: Explainability (also referred to as "interpretability") is the concept that a machine learning model and its output can be explained in a way that "makes sense" to a human being at an acceptable level.

This glossary provides a foundation, but I recommend adding to it as you discover new terms and concepts in the ever-evolving field of AI. Additionally, consider providing examples or brief use-cases for some terms to make the glossary even more helpful for beginners.

Examples Or Brief "Use-Cases" to Enhance Understanding by Beginners of AI Concepts for a Selection of the Glossary above

Adding examples or brief use-cases can greatly enhance the understanding of AI concepts for beginners. Here are examples or use-cases for a selection of the terms from the glossary:

1. AI (Artificial Intelligence): Examples include voice assistants like Siri and Alexa, which understand and respond to spoken commands, and recommendation systems like those used by Netflix or Amazon to suggest movies or products based on past behaviour.

2. Machine Learning (ML): A use-case is email filtering, where ML algorithms learn to classify emails into spam and not-spam by recognizing patterns in the data.

3. Deep Learning: An example is facial recognition technology used in smartphones for security purposes, which relies on deep learning algorithms to identify individual features.

4. Neural Network: Use-cases include handwriting recognition used by postal services to sort letters based on the written addresses, by analysing the shapes and patterns of the letters.

5. Supervised Learning: An example is a credit scoring system that predicts the likelihood of a default based on past financial behaviour of the individual.

6. Unsupervised Learning: Market basket analysis in retail, where the system identifies products often bought together without prior labelling of the data.

7. Reinforcement Learning: Self-driving cars use reinforcement learning to make decisions on the road, learning over time from the consequences of actions in a simulated environment.

8. Natural Language Processing (NLP): Chatbots use NLP to understand and respond to human queries in a natural way, improving customer service experiences.

9. Computer Vision: Automated medical diagnosis systems use computer vision to analyse images like X-

rays or MRIs to help detect diseases like cancer at early stages.

10. GAN (Generative Adversarial Network): A use-case is creating realistic-looking images or videos for entertainment or educational purposes, such as generating new artworks or simulating historical events.

11. Data Mining: Retail companies use data mining to analyse customer purchase history and behaviour to improve product recommendations and targeted marketing.

12. Bias: An example is a hiring tool that unintentionally favours candidates from a particular demographic because it was trained on data reflecting past hiring biases.

13. Ethics in AI: Developing autonomous weapons systems raises ethical questions about the delegation of life-and-death decisions to machines.

14. Robotics: Use-cases include manufacturing robots in car assembly lines that perform repetitive tasks with

precision or medical robots that assist in surgery with high accuracy.

15. Big Data: Analysing social media data to understand public sentiment about a product or political issue, enabling real-time responses from businesses or governments.

16. Cloud Computing: Services like Google Docs allow users to store documents in the cloud and access them from anywhere, facilitating collaboration and data sharing.

17. IoT (Internet of Things): Smart home devices like thermostats that learn a homeowner's preferences and adjust settings automatically to improve comfort and energy efficiency.

These examples should help beginners grasp how AI concepts are applied in real-world situations, making the abstract more tangible and understandable.

ALL BOOKS PUBLISHED BY AUTHOR OF THIS BOOK

These books can be viewed/ bought by following the link below to the Amazon site:

https://selvasmail.com/selvasbooks

Alternatively, should you wish to view the books on your phone or tablet, you could scan the barcode below, which will also take you direct to the Amazon site.

Scan me

BOOKS ON WELLNESS & HEALTH (7 BOOKS)

BOOKS ON ALZHEIMER'S & DEMENTIA (5 BOOKS)

 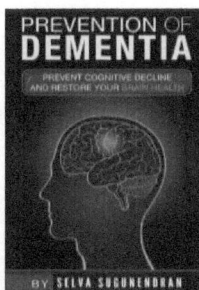 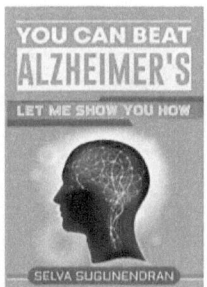

BOOKS ON SUCCESS (5 Books)

CHRISTIAN BOOKS (15 BOOKS)

NEW ADDITIONS

APPENDICES

1. WEBSITE LINKS

http://MyChristianLifestyle.org

http://BlessMeLord.com

http://HealMeLord.today

http://CreationEvolutionAndScience.com

http://AIRoboticsForGood.com

http://DementiaAdvice.care

http://HowToLeadAVibrantLifeWithAlzheimers.com

http://PreventDelayReverseAlzheimers.com

2. CONTACT LINKS:

The Author: Selva@MyChristianLifestyle.org

All Books by Author Available on Amazon:
http://Books.Selvamedia.com

www.ingramcontent.com/pod-product-compliance
Lightning Source LLC
Chambersburg PA
CBHW031415210526
45464CB00005B/1899